True Tales of a Cowboy
The Life and Times of Dale Sims

by
Marilyn Magee
from interviews with **Dale Sims**

Pen and Sword Publishers Ltd.
www.penandswordpublishing.com

Table of Contents

Foreword

The elderly gentleman sat at the dining table, bow-legged and lanky, telling me in his bona fide Texas drawl the stories of his childhood. His eyes sparkled as his mind transported him back in time to the "good old days" when he was a boy working like a grown man. I listened so intently to his story that, at times, I forgot to pick up my pen and capture his words. Enthralled by his stories, I found myself envisioning the details he was painting on the canvas of my mind as he spoke.

So begins the *True Tales of a Cowboy - The Life and Times of Dale Sims*.

Marilyn Magee

Foreword

Acknowledgements

Special thanks to Kelly Baldwin of Angry Martian Productions – Photo Restoration & Retouching for cleaning up the old photos for us.

Thanks also to editors Lin Bayhi and Linda Lane for their professional polishing of our original manuscript and to Pen and Sword Publishers Ltd. for creating the new layout with updated content and placement of photos.

My brother Joe, my dad
and me (the little tyke)

Grandpa and Grandma Sims
my uncle and brother

Chapter One
Childress, Texas

I was born in 1928 in Childress, Texas. There were 10 of us kids—three girls and seven boys—so we did whatever we could to help out, and that included workin'. My brothers and I worked any way we could to make money. Sometimes it was pickin' cotton, and other times we'd work at ranches, doin' all the dirty work. I quit school in fifth grade when I

My dad, 'is huntin' dogs, an' some of us boys

was about 12 years old. Some of the other boys did, too, and we went to work. The girls stayed in school longer.

When I was a young'un, my dad had huntin' dogs. Him and 'is friends'd take 'em out, an' at night you could hear them critters afar off.

Chapter Two
Learnin' to Work

I started workin' every Wednesday when I was about 12 years old. Four of us boys—me, two of my brothers, and another guy—flanked calves, workin' at a sale barn.

The Army bought horses and mules and shipped 'em to Texas on a train. About one mile west of the train station was the stockyard, and a mile east of the station was the sale barn. So us boys would git horses in the stockyard and take 'em to the sale barn. When we got 'em there, we got the cockle burrs

out of their manes and tails and then cleaned 'em up with kerosene—we called it coal oil. We had to put 'em in a gate so they couldn't kick us. Pay was about a dollar per day, sometimes only fifty cents.

We also worked for a man named Martin, who had a ranch about 12 miles north of town. The old man lived in town, but he would come and eat with us. Six to eight boys worked there at a time. We had a bunkhouse and a cook and ever'thing. Martin was the first rancher I worked for, but later I worked for another one named Roy.

One time Martin came up to me and said, "Dale, I bought a good horse at the sale last night, and I want you to ride 'im." He was a big, stout roan, a good-lookin' horse.

"I'll ride 'em," I said, "but you gotta call the guy and find out what's wrong with 'im. There's a hole in 'im somewhere [something not right with him]."

A couple days later, Martin came back. "I found out what's the matter with 'im. When you're ropin' and you raise up the rope, he'll buck you off."

One mornin' I decided to ride 'im, but I wanted my brother Ray, who was two years younger than me, to come with me just in case I needed help. So we was out ridin' and came across some three-year-old heifers. I told Ray it was time to test the roan. We were near a bank when one of the heifers broke into a run. I roped 'er around the neck and got 'er front legs. I couldn't have roped 'er better, but that dumb cotton picker I was ridin' blowed hisself up. I jumped off, and the heifer hit 'im hard, jerkin' 'im down. The roan got all rolled up in the rope; then she unwound 'im the same way. I tell you, he learnt his lesson. After that, I had no problems with 'im.

Most times when we was workin' the ranches, we had to doctor calves that had screw worms. That's them worms what got on 'em when they was bloody or got castrated. One time—I guess I was about thirteen then—I got on my horse, and I had some piggin' string on the saddle. Well, goin' out across the range I saw a calf that needed doctorin'. We run up on that calf, and I dropped 'im just like that and doctored 'im right up. That roan was a good calvin' horse. We went on workin' on ranches for a few years that way.

Once I saw a bunch of buzzards flyin' overhead and thought, *something's dead*. It weren't dead though. A big old Hereford steer got his head stuck in the fork of a tree. I looked around and saw a big limb 'bove 'im, so I threw a rope over 'is head and made a halter out of it by puttin' a hondoo [knot] under 'is chin. I tied it up over his muzzle and pulled away with my horse. The steer bucked backwards, and 'is head lifted up out o' that tree. He was so tired from tryin' to git loose he didn't try to run off or nothin'. I doctored him up best I could and told 'em back at the ranch where he was. They hauled him food and water for a while, and he done all right after that, I guess.

The guy we was workin' for, Martin, had brought in some cattle. The stockyard where the train was goin' to let 'em off was better'n six miles from the ranch. But this time there was too many of 'em for the stockyard to hold. I guess there was maybe 50 to 100 per car. So Martin hollered at James, 'is nephew, to go with 'im. "We'll go down the road and slow down them steers," he yelled. I tried to tell him his idea wouldn't work, but he just gave me a scoldin' cuz he thought I was just some dumb kid. What did I know? I knowed them steers was tired of bein' on that train, and they was cold and wanted to run so's they could warm up. We went down the road, and about 300 of them steers took off runnin' and broke the fence down.

My buddy Freddy Cardell and I went to find the ones that took off and bring 'em back. We'd put 'em in a trailer and bring 'em over to the ranch. Sometimes we'd find one at that ranch or at t'other ranch, and we'd go git 'em.

That winter, I worked at a feed store and did anything else I could find. Then in the spring, I went to work in Lazare, Texas, about sixteen miles from Childress. I still worked for Roy then, and I remember when we went to a cow sale at Quanah. One particular day we went to town, and he took to nippin' a bottle and got drunk. He went and bought a mare, so we run her up into the truck and took her to the ranch.

Roy, knowin' he bought things when he hit the bottle too much, asked the next morning, "So what did I buy?"

I said, "You bought a tiger." That mare was a wild one. I got her haltered and tied her to a fence for three or four days. 'Course, I took her food and water, and I finally got 'er to where

I could ride her. I rode 'er probably twelve or fifteen times. She had an "OX" brand on her, so I called her Oxydol. [Oxydol, a laundry detergent created by Proctor and Gambel in 1927, sponsored a soap opera, *Ma Perkins*, that debuted on the radio on December 4, 1933.]

One day we was tyin' some fence stays. I tied her to my belt loop so's she wouldn't run off. I bent over with a pair of bull nose pliers, and she bit me on the back. I was a scrawny kid and didn't have much meat on me then, but I heard her teeth clench t'gither real hard when she bit me. Man, that mare was mean! She could kick you from four feet away. If someone was standin' nearby, she would ease on over to them and kick 'em! She even did that while I was ridin' 'er. Everybody knew to stay away from 'er.

We had to go doctor some cattle. I went to git an old yeller horse, but he was limpin'. So I rode Oxydol. She'd been in the wheat field for two weeks and had a big belly, but I didn't think nothin' of it. That was on a Tuesday. I worked her hard that day, and she got in the mud up past her feet. I roped two heifers, got 'em doctored, and set her loose in the corral when we was done.

On Wednesday, we went to the sale barn, where we sometimes worked for twenty-four hours straight and only earned three dollars. Later that day, Roy asked me, "How much do you want for Oxydol?"

"Thirty-seven-fifty, just like I been sayin'."

"Thirty-seven-fifty for both of 'em?" he shot back.

"Thirty-seven-fifty if'n there were three of 'em." I didn't know she was pregnant, but Roy knew. She had a colt and lived through it. I kept her, but I never got on her again for six months. I wouldn't have worked her so hard had I knowed she was carryin'. I finally sold her to a gal named Jeanne, who won barrel races on her later on.

One time Roy was gonna ship cows. About a hundred of 'em were driven up to the corral, and he pointed out one of 'em to me and said, "You see her? She's a dry cow, but when we put her in the corral, she'll go to the back side and jump the fence—always does. You go on back there, and when she does, rope her." So I rode that big yellow horse, and I roped her good. But that big horse jerked her down real hard and her leg broke, so we got her butchered. Roy said to me, "Dale, as long as I got a cow, you got a job." His mom, on the other hand, saw what happened and said, "You keep him around, and you ain't gonna have any cows for very long."

We worked all that summer and fall. The next spring, of course, there were some calves that needed doctorin'. One of the ranchers came by my parent's place and took us out there to work for him. I took my lunch, and we doctored calves all day. He had a big paint horse. I loved ropin' off that horse. I roped about twelve to fifteen calves ever'day. We spent three weeks doctorin' screw worms.

In the winter, I usually worked at the feed store. But this winter, a guy who had a ranch about 65 miles from Childress wanted us to work on the Hossick Ranch. I needed a pair of chaps first, and so I had Paul [owner of a saddle shop] make me a pair. He had 'em just about done when we got that new job. And do you know he finished 'em for me that day so's I could start workin'. The guys teased me about my new chaps: "What'er ya gonna do, deliver feed in 'em?"

None of us had a car, so one of the guys from the ranch loaded up our saddles and gear in his vehicle, and gave us a ride.

My nephew and
my brother Duane

Chapter Three
The Dumbest Horse in the World

We went up to one more ranch on Sunday afternoon late in the fall. We were just sittin' around, and the foreman said, "Go out to the corral and pick out the horses you're gonna ride. Pick three each. Then go to the colt corral and pick one colt each."

When we got to the colt corral, we just looked at each other and asked him, "How old are these colts?"

"Seven."

We looked at each other again. What they done was ride 'em three times around the corral and call 'em broke. But that ain't broke. When they was turned out to pasture and got rode for three or four days in a row, then they'd be broke. Ray, myself, Joe, and Oscar from Childress went to pick out our colts. We'd ride a colt every fourth day. I caught my colt and got 'im saddled. He kicked at me and broke loose. I caught 'im again and put a bow saw on 'im, and the foreman told me I was goin' to need all the long reins I had on 'im. I got 'im jerked down and broke, but he tried to buck me off ever'day. He was so dumb he couldn't learn nothin'. I went to the tank (a lake) to head 'em north. If you know anythin' about cattle, you know they'll head straight to the water tank. We rode in pairs, Ray and I got to the tank first, and the other guys brought their cattle, too. I hated to git off my horse, but I needed to. There was six to eight inches of water and about two inches of mud. Do you know that dirty cotton picker kicked and drug me through that tank? If I coulda drowned 'im, I'da done it. There was a huckleberry tree nearby with a limb that hung down, so I tied him up high in a tree. When he kicked up, his back legs went down, and he ended up hanging there, fightin' it. So I just let 'im for a while. But this dumb horse couldn't learn anythin'.

The foreman come in and said, "Where's your horse?"

"He's a hangin' in a tree," I told 'im.

"You better go cut him loose. It's a long way to carry your saddle."

So I did. I woulda done it anyways, but I had to teach that dumb cotton picker a lesson.

Sometimes the neighboring ranchers would send two guys over to git their cattle out of our rancher's pasture. One of 'em was a black guy, and one time we rode t'gither in the mornin'. About thirty minutes into the ride, he says to me, "Dale, I forgot my chewin' tobacca. You got any?" I had some, and so I handed it to him. He wouldn't take it. He didn't want to touch my tobacca because he was black and I was white. He said for me to just cut 'im a piece of the plug, so I cut it and gave 'im half. We rode into the cattle. A big steer broke into a run, and he said, "That's one of ours." (He saw the brand.) He got 'im roped and jerked 'im three or four times, and I stretched 'im out. When he got the rope off his head, the steer went back to the bunch and just stayed there. He didn't want to mess with that guy again.

When it was time to eat, we went to the cook shack in threes so's there'd always be guys in the pasture. This particular day, we were the last bunch to go. When we got back to the cook shack, he (the black guy) said to me and Ray, "Would one of you guys fix me a plate an' bring it over here?"

I told him, "I absolutely will not. If you're good enough to work with, you're good enough to eat with."

I can't remember his name now. He was about 30, and I was about 15. He called me "sir." I couldn't believe it. I liked that guy a lot. He was a real cowboy—I knowed that by just seein' 'im rope that steer.

One guy that came over to work with us said his name was Weeks. I asked him if he was any relation to Billy Weeks. He said, "Yeah, he's my uncle." Billy Weeks was a famous horseman, but

I don't know if this guy was really his nephew or not. There was another cowboy I'd heard of by the name of Guy Weeks, and he could've been the same boy that rode on that ranch. Guy rode in the Cheyenne Frontier Days Rodeo in the '50s.

When we was done at that ranch, we went home for a spell. My friend at that time was T.L.; I ran around with him and his sister. I was goin' with his sister for a while, and then the family moved to San Angelo. I stayed with 'em for about two weeks and got a job workin' in a factory. I didn't like it, so I quit. I was told her family moved to San Angelo to git her away from me. Don't know if that was true or not, but I left. I didn't want to work full time on ranches. I had my sights on another way of life: the rodeo and bulldoggin'.

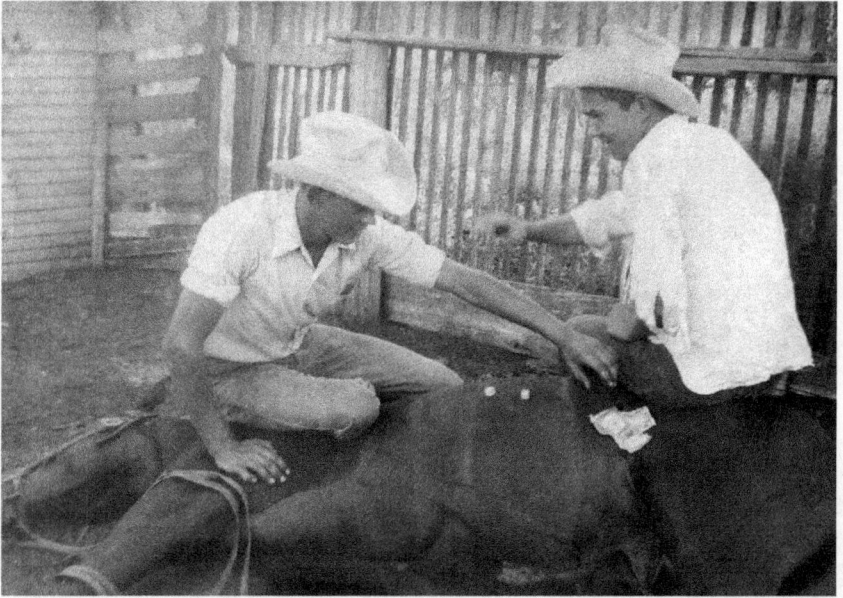

Me and my friend TL playing dice on Eli

Chapter Four
Bulldoggin' Bug

That same year, a guy named Philips won bulldoggin'. I wanted to go learn somethin' at his place, but he never did teach me. So I learned bulldoggin' by myself. I bought a steer and turned him out

Us guys spendin'
our money in town

in a wheat field. My buddy Freddy and I ran that steer ever'day, once a day. Bulldoggin' took brute strength because you'd just jump off your horse and throw the steer down.

The winner was the one who did it fastest. It paid good if you won.

When I was 16, I tried ridin' a bull. I stayed on for six seconds cuz that was all I could handle. I felt my insides git all tore up.

That night I was stayin' in a hotel in Pampah, Texas. I was with a family whose kids were in the rodeo, too. I asked 'em to take me to the highway so's I could hitchhike home. It was about 125 miles away, but I was so sick I didn't care. I hitched a ride back to Childress, and the next day they took me to the hospital. The doctor said I had the polio. Now I don't believe I had the polio; I was just all tore up inside from that bull ride. I was in the hospital for six weeks. They wrapped me up in a wool army blanket and kept on feedin' me water to just sweat the sickness out of me.

When I got out of the hospital, I went and stayed with my sister, Elora. She had an extra bedroom. There was a very nice lady in town named Della Layton (Freddy's aunt), who owned the local movie theater She looked out for me. She'd come in to Elora's place and bring groceries. Della told her to feed me three steaks a day so's I could fatten up after bein' so sick. She was about 40 or 50 years old back then, but she'd come to visit with me while I healed up. She'd pull up her britches, sit right down on the bed, and we'd just talk. We would talk about ever'thing. She could carry on a good conversation. Della let us kids go to the movies fer nothin'. She told them girls who worked there that if'n we didn't have no money to let us in fer free.

Chapter Five
Leavin' Texas

In 1949, I came to Colorado to be a worker at a livery stable in Estes Park. Back in those days, busses would bring people to Estes Park from Boulder. There was only one way up—on the bus. They'd wanna go horseback ridin', so we took 'em. One time there was a bus load of girls. Do you know those girls tipped me $20? I lived on tips all summer 'cause I didn't git paid till the season was over. We stayed in the bunkhouse at the stable, and we ate at the Chalet. That's where

Some of the Sims family

I met Ruth. She was a maid at the hotel and about 17 or 18 years old. Come wintertime, I went back to Childress, and she went back to Boulder. But I told her I liked it up at Estes Park and I'd come back. So I did.

It was about that time that Ruth met Lucille Hyatt, whose dad was a horse shoer (some people call 'em a farrier). Lucille, a young gal, went with us to all the rodeos.

Chapter Six
Marryin' Ruth and Startin' a Family

We got married in 1950, and we lived in Boulder. I got me a job in construction, workin' for a man named Frank. A couple of years after we were married, our good friend Lucille moved in with us. She was like our first daughter. Then in 1955, our own daughter, Becky, was born, and Debbie came along in 1960. We didn't take the girls to the rodeo if it was a hot spell. We had a couple of ladies that would watch 'em. One of the ladies, Miriam Montgomery, owned a dairy across the road from us. The other gal was Jenny, Frank's wife.

Later, as the girls learned to ride, they wanted to go to horse shows and run the barrels. So we let 'em for awhile, but the parents of the other kids would git all upset if their kid didn't win, so the girls decided to ride for the enjoyment of it and not in competition.

Ruth and our "adopted" daughter, Lucille

29

Pro-Rodeo Rider Dale Sims in 1966
at the Denver Stock Show

Chapter Seven
Rodeo Days

I did ever'thing 'cept plumbin' and wirin' at the construction company where I worked. At night, after work, I bulldogged. On weekends, we went to rodeos nearby. I was in the Boulder Pow Wow. It was on 28th Street back then, where the Y.M.C.A building is now. A man donated that land to the Boulder Pow Wow Committee, but somehow the city ended up with it. Almost all the champions rode in that pow wow, includin' Billy Weeks. I went to rodeos in Cheyenne and Pueblo on weekends. Ruth went to nearly all of 'em with me. The top fifteen guys went a short go-around. The Cowboy Rodeo Association lost the records in a fire, so I don't think there's anythin' left with my name on it. I worked five days a week at a regular job to make sure we had everything we needed. My family always came first.

Me bulldoggin' an itty bitty steer • circa 1952

I owned a stable up in Nederlands in 1960, but later I sold it. In '69, I built a house in Boulder Heights, then sold it in '70 and moved out of Colorado.

Dale on horse in front of stable

Chapter Eight
On the Road Again

We took the camper and just started drivin'. We ended up in Klamath Falls, Oregon, where we stayed long enough for Becky to graduate. Then we moved to Montana. We were near a town called Manhattan on 10 acres. Debbie graduated durin' the 15 years we lived in Montana. We had a housewarmin' with the fire department. (In other words, the house burnt down.) But the insurance paid for it. A real estate guy called and wanted to sell the property for us and said he had an offer. We thought about it some and told 'im to double it and we'd take the offer. He said okay, so we sold it. We moved back to Colorado after the fire to 30th and Valmont in Boulder. Our friends told us to come on down, and they had a trailer we could live in. So we stayed there until I built a house on St. Vrain Road in Boulder.

Ruth and me with our
daughters, Becky and Debbie

Chapter Nine
The Rodeo Goes on...

R uth passed away in 2001 from a bad heart. It was a diffi-
cult time for us. I sure miss her. Lovin' the same woman yer entire life is a beautiful thing. At first you don't
think the rodeo will go on...but it does. Life goes on, the rodeo
continues, you pull yerself up by the bootstraps, and you git up
an' go. Today, I live in Berthoud, Colo. Thankfully, the girls are
nearby. Debbie lives in Berthoud, and Becky lives in the east
end of Longmont.

Mom and Dad

Chapter 10
Reminiscin'

Now, I enjoy goin' to the rodeo and watchin' the new riders, the young ones related to me and those that I rode with back in the good ole days. In those days, our entertainment was laughin' at each other whenever we wrecked (got bucked off a horse). We never got paid much, but it sure kept us out of trouble. And that was worth a lot!

One time, I knew this guy whose wife just had a baby. When she got the baby to sleep and laid him down, this plane would fly over the house and wake the baby. It did that ever'day. Do you know she got out a .22 and shot holes in the wings of that plane? Needless to say, they never flew over and woke up that baby again!

Another time, when we was in Oklahoma, we was haulin' a horse in the back of a pickup truck. After passin' a gas station, the guy I was with says to me, "Dale, I think I shoulda put gas in back there." We ran out. Wouldn't you know it? Right there in the middle of the field was a tractor and a Oklahoma credit card (siphoning hose). We left some money an' a note, thankin' 'em for the gas.

One of the places I loved goin' was Cheyenne. It was one of the most popular rodeos, always bustlin' with people. The excitement in the air just made yer hair stand on end. That was the best place ever.

Many people have stories to tell the young'uns, but they never do. I have had a lot of people tell me to write my stories down, to tell others about my life as a cowboy—my life full of adventures and good friends and family—and so I did.

The Sims Family

Parents: William (Bill) and Sadie Sims, all children born at
home
Siblings: Mildred – 5 children
Clifford – 2 children
Morgan – married a woman with 2 children; they
had 1 more together
Elora – 1 child
Ollie – 1 child with first husband, killed in army;
2 with second husband
J.B. – Never married
Joe – 2 children
Dale – Born in 1928 – no birth certificate, record
only in family Bible; 2 children; wife – Ruth
Ray – 3 children, 2 boys and a girl; one son was a
rodeo clown bullfighter.
Duane – Surviving brother as of June 2009, still in
Childress, Texas. 1 child – boy

The Boulder Rodeo

A tradition that would span fifty years began in 1934—the Boulder Pay Dirt Pow Wow. Started as an effort to distract Boulder County Metal Mining Association employees from the harsh realities of the Great Depression, it became an instant hit. Co-sponsored by the Boulder Chamber of Commerce, its grounds sat between 28th and 30th streets, Mapleton, and Pearl; and it grew from small beginnings as county fair contests to an annual rodeo drawing professional contenders such as Dale Sims and others to the major event.

In 1979, the land was sold and the name changed to Boulder Valley Pow Wow. It moved to South Boulder Road near Louisville but failed to thrive after the relocation. In 1984, it went into foreclosure, shutting the door on an era that had lasted half a century.

Dale Sims bulldoggin' • circa 1951

www.ingramcontent.com/pod-product-compliance
Lightning Source LLC
Chambersburg PA
CBHW021121020426
42331CB00004B/579